万圣节

Customs, Traditions and Landmarks |
Non-Fiction Series

Copyright © 2022 by Level Learning, INC. and Washington Yu Ying PCS™
Original and Edited Text Copyright © 2022 by Washington Yu Ying PCS™

All rights reserved. No part of this book in whole or part may be reproduced without written permission from the publisher.

Published by Level Learning, INC.

Content Contributors:
Washington Yu Ying PCS™
Level Learning - Ya-Ching Chang

Illustrations by: Josh Taira

Leveling classification based on Level Learning standard. For full description, visit www.levellearning.com

ISBN 978-1-64040-012-2
Simplified Chinese Edition

About Level Learning:
Level Learning provides a literacy focused curriculum specifically designed for K-12 Chinese as a Second Language classrooms. Our program offers 20 levels of specific and detailed objectives, leveled texts and passages, mastery-based online assessment, and analytics to enable data-driven instruction. Level Learning reading curriculum for both literature and informational text emphasize grammar and comprehension skills to help teachers develop confident and independent Chinese language readers. The non-fiction series of books are specifically designed to support our informational text course based on multiple national standards. To learn more about our entire offering, visit www.levellearning.com

About Washington Yu Ying PCS™:
Washington Yu Ying PCS is a Mandarin English dual language immersion International Baccalaureate (IB) World school. Yu Ying's mission is to inspire and prepare young people to create a better world by challenging them to reach their full potential in a nurturing Chinese/English educational environment. Yu Ying's comprehensive IB, dual immersion curriculum equips students with global competencies for success in the real world. As a leader in immersion education, Yu Ying is determined to advance Chinese language programs and global citizenry education by helping other schools create and strengthen their Chinese programs. For more information, email: products@washingtonyuying.org

			十月			
星期一	星期二	星期三	星期四	星期五	星期六	星期日
	1	2	3	4	5	6
7	8	9	10	11	12	13
14	15	16	17	18	19	20
21	22	23	24	25	26	27
28	29	30	31			

每年的十月三十一日是万圣节。这一天，人们会穿上特别的衣服，装扮成不同的样子。

有人会装扮成巫婆，黑漆漆的长袍，看起来特别吓人！

有人会装扮成吸血鬼，血淋淋的牙齿，看起来特别可怕！

有人会装扮成大南瓜。圆滚滚的身体，看起来特别可爱！

在这一天，人们会在家门口放一个南瓜灯笼。人们也会把房子装饰成鬼屋。

到了晚上,小朋友们会一起去邻居家要糖果。

小朋友们要说：不给糖，就捣蛋！这天晚上，小朋友们都会拿到好多的糖果。

万圣节真是一个特别的节日。

Glossary

	Pinyin	English Definition
万圣节	wàn shèng jié	Halloween
装扮	zhuāng bàn	to dress up
样子	yàng zi	appearance, look like
巫婆	wū pó	witch
黑漆漆	hēi qī qī	black
长袍	cháng páo	long robe
吓人	xià rén	to scare
吸血鬼	xī xuè guǐ	vampire
血淋淋	xiě lín lín	bloody
牙齿	yá chǐ	tooth
可怕	kě pà	scary
南瓜	nán guā	pumpkin
圆滚滚	yuán gǔn gǔn	round, plump
身体	shēn tǐ	body
可爱	kě ài	cute

	Pinyin	English Definition
灯笼	dēng long	lantern
装饰	zhuāng shì	to decorate
鬼屋	guǐ wū	haunted house
邻居	lín jū	neighbor
糖果	táng guǒ	candy
捣蛋	dǎo dàn	mischief
特别	tè bié	special

www.ingramcontent.com/pod-product-compliance
Lightning Source LLC
Chambersburg PA
CBHW041224070526
44584CB00001B/80